365 DAYS
OF
LAUGHTER

Lizzie Cornwall

summersdale

Summersdale Publishers Ltd
46 West Street
Chichester
West Sussex
PO19 1RP
UK

www.summersdale.com

Printed and bound in the Czech Republic

ISBN: 978-1-84953-545-8

Substantial discounts on bulk quantities of Summersdale books are available to corporations, professional associations and other organisations. For details contact Nicky Douglas by telephone: +44 (0) 1243 756902, fax: +44 (0) 1243 786300 or email: nicky@summersdale.com.

To..

From..

JANUARY

New Year's Day: Join all the other daredevils and go for a New Year's Day dip in the sea. Dress up for the occasion as a mermaid or your favourite type of fish.

 It's back to the office today for many. Take all your unwanted Christmas gifts to work and set up a market stall at your desk. Drum up business with cries of *'Anything for a tenner'*, *'You want it for a fiver?'* and *'You're robbing me!'*

Start a juggling club, introducing something new and more adventurous to juggle with each week – fruit, shoes, cushions…

 Laugh as much as possible today. Turn every amusing moment into a raucous belly laugh – you'll find it's infectious.

 Purchase a diary and turn it into a laughter journal, writing down something funny that has happened each day. It could be an overheard conversation that made you giggle, a new joke or even a dream you had.

Go for a walk in the hills with a rambling group and yodel on reaching every summit.

 Get dressed in your partner's/flatmate's clothes and see how long it takes them to notice.

 Ask everyone you meet today to tell you their favourite joke. Spread the laughter by matching theirs with one of yours.

Scuttle sideways round the supermarket like a crab; make pincer movements with your hands when picking up groceries.

 Invest in a popgun for watching films in the long winter evenings and aim your shot at the baddies when they appear on-screen.

 See how often you can get the word 'woof' into a conversation. *'Woof, I would like a woofing milkshake and woof-woof fries, please. Woof.'*

A day without laughter is a day wasted.

Charlie Chaplin

If you have good thoughts
they will shine out of your
face like sunbeams and
you will always
look lovely.

Roald Dahl

Spin like a whirling dervish.

 Have a spacehopper race with a competitive friend – the loser has to complete a dare!

 Launch into 'I Want to Break Free' by Queen the next time you're undertaking a job that you don't want to do.

Put two gobstoppers in your mouth before having a conversation with your best mate.

 Sign up now to take part in a charity fun run or skydive later in the year and start preparing for it. Your first step is to think up the most outrageous outfit you can wear.

 Pack some edible pants in your partner's packed lunch.

Laughter is the closest thing to the grace of God.

Karl Barth

I am thankful for laughter,
except when milk comes
out of my nose.

Woody Allen

Make balloon animals, then name each one and give them a good home.

 Write funny messages on the dirt on cars, e.g. *'Cleanliness is next to godliness'* and *'You missed a bit'*.

 On a dull, dreary day, wear rose-tinted sunglasses and the brightest clothes in your wardrobe.

 Learn some tricks with a yo-yo.

Watch an old episode of your favourite sitcom then, straight away, start writing a sequel. Make it as funny as you can.

 The next time someone asks for more froth on their cappuccino, place a straw in the coffee and blow into it.

 The world record for rocking non-stop in a rocking chair is 453 hours and 40 minutes. See if you can become a record-breaker.

29

National Puzzle Day: Replace words in your conversations with crossword clues, e.g. 'Can you pass me the china drinks container, three letters?'

30 Wear Dracula fangs to the dentist.

31 Don't use the stairs – slide down the bannister.

FEBRUARY

 Bring a recorder into work and perform an impromptu recital during tea break.

 Replace photos on colleagues' desks with pictures of yourself and see how long it takes them to notice.

 Wear a monocle for the day and stroke your chin every time someone speaks to you.

Earth laughs in flowers.

Ralph Waldo Emerson

I don't trust anyone who doesn't laugh.

Maya Angelou

6 If you find yourself in a downpour, get your brolly out and do a bit of *Singin' in the Rain* à la Gene Kelly.

7 Run along a crowded street with a large bunch of balloons and then let them go.

8 Wear a stick-on moustache for the day (regardless of gender) and deny all knowledge of it when people ask you about it.

FEBRUARY

 Put extra crackle in the crackling for Sunday lunch by sprinkling on some popping candy.

 Invest in some old-school joke props, such as a whoopee cushion and fake dog poo, and have hours of fun planting them in strategic places round the house or office.

 Blow a kiss to the person in the car next to you when you're stuck at the traffic lights.

Think of the silliest thing you could do right now. Do it.

 Tamper with the autocorrect function on a colleague's computer so that every time they type their name it comes up with 'Silly Sausage'.

Valentine's Day: On this romantic day, make the most of your lunch break and play a game of kiss chase – but make sure it's with a willing participant!

Don't despair if you didn't receive any Valentine's cards this year. Take the more direct approach and go speed dating, but with a twist, acting out the idiosyncrasies of a quirky film or book character.

 Moonwalk out of every room for the day – this works particularly well when exiting the boss's office or the supermarket.

17 Every time someone enters the room (at home or work) announce them as if they're a reality talent show contestant about to perform on stage, *'It's JOHN MILLER performing "FLYING WITHOUT WINGS"!'*

 18 Spoil yourself with some wind-up bath toys.

Treat today like a game show and buzz into all your conversations.

 Buy a magic wand from a toy shop and then immediately take it back, stating *'it doesn't work'*.

21

There is nothing in the
world so irresistibly
contagious as laughter
and good humour.

Charles Dickens

Life is worth living as long as there's a laugh in it.

L. M. Montgomery

23 Treat yourself and your partner to a night in a fancy hotel and spend a good portion of the evening having a pillow fight.

 24 Come up with an amusing pseudonym to use when booking tables at restaurants and signing guest books.

 25 Place a dead woodlouse in an empty matchbox and take it to work. Ask its opinion when making important executive decisions throughout the day.

Build your own drum kit with the contents of your kitchen and perform a solo for your nearest and dearest.

 Reduce your carbon footprint today with a chuckle. Instead of taking the car to work, get your rollerblades on and skate – don't forget those leg warmers.

Wear a toy gun holster belt loaded with bananas and challenge your friends to 'stick 'em up'.

Leap Day: Play leapfrog with a friend or colleague.

MARCH

 Bow or curtsey when greeting anyone and everyone for the day.

 Wear a Marie Antoinette wig to the hairdressers and request, *'Just a little off the top.'*

 Don't allow anyone into your house without the secret password, but refuse to divulge what the secret password is.

Be sure to celebrate Pancake Day with a race. Seek out the champion pancake-tosser in your neighbourhood.

 Be creative with your lunch and make a sculpture out of cheese. Take a photo of it and post it on a social networking site, encouraging others to do the same.

 Go jogging early in the morning and high-five any other joggers you come across.

 Eat a doughnut without licking your lips.

Shuffle along the floor on your bottom when moving from one room to the next.

 Invite friends over and play old-fashioned parlour games, such as charades, blind man's bluff or sardines.

 Make a playlist of the cheesiest party songs and play it on your MP3 player; make sure you do the dancing actions as you hear them.

 Play truth or dare with a group of good friends and think of some outrageous dares to perform.

The human race has only one really effective weapon and that is laughter.

Mark Twain

Laughter is the sound of the soul dancing.

Jarod Kintz

MARCH

 Try reciting the tongue twister *'I'm not a pheasant plucker'* really fast. Make sure no children are around!

 The next time someone asks you to make yourself comfortable, be it at a friend's house or a party, take them at their word and change into your pyjamas and slippers.

 Dress up the entire family as the *Where's Wally?* characters and take turns to hide in the local park.

World Sleep Day: Indulge your inner Goldilocks by insisting on trying out every bed in a furniture showroom. See how much snoring you can do before someone taps you on the shoulder.

 Find some iconic images, such as Neil Armstrong on the moon, the marriage of Prince William and Kate Middleton, etc., and superimpose your face onto the pictures, then hang them on your wall for posterity.

 Greet the new day as a cockerel would.

Always laugh when you can; it is cheap medicine.

Lord Byron

The only honest art form is laughter.

Lenny Bruce

First day of spring: Dust down that pogo stick and get jumping!

 Make a pizza portrait of your dinner guest and serve it to them.

 Write jokes on the walls before wallpapering a room so the next person decorating it has a laugh.

 Go into a building via a revolving door and revolve your way straight out again, keeping your face completely straight as you do so – save the chuckle for later.

26 Try to make everyone that you come across laugh today, but without uttering a word – use the power of the gurn!

 27 Hang from a tree like a monkey.

 28 Put on a silly voice, or use a simple voice-changer gadget and ring your friends. See who takes the longest to work out it's you.

29 Email everyone in the office and inform them that you have to go to an interview with a travelling circus — then arrive at work dressed as a clown to make it convincing.

 30 Challenge yourself to tweet a joke every half an hour on your Twitter feed for the day.

 31 Make a cardboard replica of your office and add cut-out characters to represent everyone there, then perform short plays for your own amusement.

APRIL

April Fool's Day: Treat everything you hear as if it were an April Fool's trick. 'My tea's ready? Nah, you're having me on!'

 Dress in the clothes that your teenage self would wear and go about with your hands hung at your sides telling everyone you hate them.

There is little success where there is little laughter.

Andrew Carnegie

If you can't laugh, you won't make it.

Jennifer Love Hewitt

5 Use a page of a notebook to write down funny words that amuse you: 'knuckleduster' or 'spaghettification', for example. Keep topping up the list.

6 Find a big hill and roly-poly down it. Make sure the grass has just been mowed so you're covered in cuttings.

7 Adopt a famous funny person's character for the day and base all your decisions on what this persona might do. Good names to start with – Mr T, Austin Powers and Mrs Doubtfire.

Make a habit of pausing today to remember the times when you really belly-laughed.

 Hum mood-appropriate music throughout the day, such as the *Jaws* theme tune when your boss appears, and the theme tune to *The Great Escape* when you're off out to do errands.

 Hire a tandem and go on a bike ride with a friend that makes you laugh.

Have a limbo dance competition.

 Watch some silly clips on YouTube for a good giggle, search for 'baby monkey', 'surprised bush baby' and 'piano-playing cat'.

 Apply liberal amounts of lipstick and greet everyone with a kiss so they have marks on their face.

The human eye blinks an average of 4,200,000 times a year – cut down on your blinks by winking at passers-by.

 Frame a picture of something inanimate, like a camera or a sausage, and give it pride of place on your desk or mantelpiece. When anyone asks why it's there, make up some bizarre story about how it once saved your life.

 Tie a dandelion to your wrist and use it to tell the time.

17

We're all here for a spell;
get all the good laughs
you can.

Will Rogers

At the height of laughter,
the universe is flung into
a kaleidoscope of new
possibilities.

Jean Houston

APRIL

 19 Wear Mickey Mouse ears and talk in a high-pitched voice. Try to convince strangers that's just how your voice sounds naturally.

 20 The next time someone talks down to you, bow and curtsey, saying, *'I do beg your pardon me lady/me lordship.'* Reverse out of the nearest exit.

 21 Next time you have a disagreement with someone, make up a rap about them. If it's with your partner, it could go something like: *'You're the boyfriend from hell, yo, yo, yo. You make me want to scream, just go, go, go!'*

22

Earth Day: The Earth keeps on spinning. Mark this day by spinning on your head; insist your friends do the same.

23

Shakespeare's birthday: Channel the brilliance of the Bard and stalk the streets in tights, ruff and codpiece, shouting, 'Forsooth' and 'Out, damned spot!'

24 Wear your clothes back to front and walk backwards.

 25 Create a poking device from desk detritus and use it to stroke your colleague's face to get their attention.

 26 Glide your way round the supermarket while perching on the back of a shopping trolley, but be mindful of other shoppers!

Take your most cherished cuddly toy out for dinner. Be sure to order for them because they might be a little shy.

 Introduce your invisible friend to your mates in the pub and insist they buy them a pint too.

Laughter is the sun that drives the winter from the human face.

Victor Hugo

It seems that laughter needs an echo.

Henri Bergson

MAY

May Day: Two words: morris dancing! Cover yourself in bells, skip around and hit sticks together!

Every time you have to say 'no' today, whinny like a horse and say 'neigh'.

People-watch on your local high street. Make up funny backstories about people you like the look of.

 Wear a utility belt and fill it with biscuits – be sure to offer them round.

World Laughter Day (first Sunday in May): Think of your own catchphrase and see how often you can slip it into conversation. Make it as random as you can, such as: 'It was the sprouts, officer!' or 'You saying I've got monkey eyes?'

Sing 'Edelweiss' from *The Sound of Music* as you shuffle on your bum up the stairs before going to bed.

 Liven up a trip to the cinema and dress in something relating to the film you are seeing. For example, wear a wetsuit and flippers for an aquatic adventure, period costume for the latest bodice-ripper or paint yourself blue for *The Smurfs* or *Avatar*.

 Take your cat for a walk.

Pull on a black unitard and white gloves and communicate using the art of mime for the day.

 The average person has over 1,460 dreams a year; write down your funniest and revisit them for a laugh.

 At your office, put a sign on the water cooler that reads *'Do not feed the piranhas!'*

 Perform a recital with a comb and some tissue paper at the next local talent night.

Laughter is the magic
that disperses clouds and
creates sunshine in
the soul.

Richelle E. Goodrich

We can't all be comedians,
some people have to do
the laughing.

Mokokoma Mokhonoana

Organise a gymkhana, but with hobby horses.

 Book a bouncy castle and a ball pool for your next birthday. It doesn't matter how old you're going to be.

 Go into a pound shop and insist on asking the staff how much things cost.

 Stick your face in a chocolate fountain.

Make your own pet rock: give him goggle eyes and pretend to feed him olives.

 Wear your wedding finery on your wedding anniversary, even if it's a work day.

 If you're camping this year, play this fun game: see who can get dressed quickest while remaining completely horizontal in their sleeping bag.

Avoid the gaps in the pavement when walking through town.

 Eat a cupcake without using your hands.

 Turn the light off every time you leave a room, even if there are people in there.

Put small cubes of cheese next to a colleague's computer mouse.

 Build a car or fort out of cardboard boxes and post a picture of yourself in it on a social networking site.

 Pretend to put sales callers on hold by playing music, preferably 'Patience' by Take That, for at least half an hour.

It is of immense
importance to learn to
laugh at ourselves.

Katherine Mansfield

What soap is to the body, laughter is to the soul.

Yiddish proverb

Play hide and seek with a co-worker. Whoever is found first must make the tea.

 It takes 492 seconds for sunlight to reach the Earth – don't waste time, brighten up your day with a walk in the sunshine.

The average person laughs 15 times a day. Who wants to be average?

 Place a gnome in a good friend's back garden so it's the first thing they see when they open the curtains in the morning.

Everybody laughs the same in every language because laughter is a universal connection.

Yakov Smirnoff

Laughter gives us distance. It allows us to step back from an event, deal with it and then move on.

Bob Newhart

Start a comical book club, where you only read books that are funny. Rate them on how humorous they are and recite the best lines out loud to each other.

 Try to break a record for charity. It could be the number of times you can belch in a minute or how many doughnuts you can eat.

 Wolf-whistle builders as you walk past them.

Play Chip Jenga. Chunky chips work best.

 Print out a life-size picture of Brad Pitt's face and stick it to the passenger window of your car. Watch as fans, young and old, become hysterical as you drive past.

 When you've bought some new bed linen, take it out of its packet and dress yourself in it.

Make the names in your phone's contacts list more outrageous: Hugh Jass, Ron Number, Chris P. Crumb.

 Smear mud on your face, throw on a vest and run round the house pretending you're in an action film.

 Stick a pencil behind your ear and try to draw/write with it while it's lodged there.

Rather than use the door, use the window of your car to get in and out of the vehicle, like Bo and Luke do in *The Dukes of Hazzard*.

 Wear a ballgown to lunch.

 Pick the most suggestive-looking vegetables at the supermarket. It'll brighten up the weekly shop.

 Draw a tattoo on your face before an important work meeting.

He who has laughter on his side has no need of proof.

Theodor W. Adorno

The person who can bring the spirit of laughter into a room is indeed blessed.

Bennett Cerf

20

Midsummer's Eve: put on a donkey mask and ask everyone to call you 'Bottom'.

21

Summer Solstice: It's going to be a long day, so resolve to stay in and watch all your favourite comedy films.

Ring up a friend with some juicy gossip and have a good belly laugh.

 Take a teddy bear for a stroll in a baby sling.

 Make up ridiculous excuses for getting out of doing the chores: *'Rubber gloves make me come out in hives!'*

I would put belly-laughing at the top of my highlights list. They always say that laughter is the best medicine.

Carol Vorderman

Laughter is, after speech, the chief thing that holds society together.

Max Eastman

27 Take your skipping rope to work and do some furious skipping beside your desk at break time.

 28 Fill a room in your house with balloons and invite friends round to jump on them.

 29 Speak like Yoda for the day. Very amusing it is!

 30 Become the neighbourhood cat whisperer – stare at a cat when you see one, then whisper to it.

JULY

National Motivation Day (UK): Organise a fun motivational event at work such as an open-mic afternoon where everyone can perform their favourite jokes.

 It's summer and your pets are moulting. Gather all the fur that has accumulated on the carpets and furniture and weave it into a beard for your beloved.

Relive those school sports day memories with a silly sports day in the park – the sack race, egg-and-spoon race and three-legged race are compulsory.

 Blow a cream horn.

 Create a 'funny board' at home. Pin up and attach things that you find hilarious – anything at all from naughty postcards to rude-sounding food labels.

It's holiday season. Start your own impromptu sightseeing tour in your town, pointing out silly things amongst the local historical facts. *'A famous playwright lived here and at this very spot, some three weeks ago, I had the misfortune of treading on a large slug while wearing my brand new sandals.'*

 Rub a bottle of fake tan into your skin and try to convince people that you spent the night on a sunbed.

 While your partner/flatmate is asleep, decorate their face with make-up.

Laughter can bring a new perspective.

Christopher Durang

Though the clown is often deadpan, he is a connoisseur of laughter.

Mel Gussow

Draw smiley faces on all the items in your fridge.

 On a sunny day, get your friends round and have a water fight. When you're soaked through, sit down and make bum prints on your patio.

 Wear Victorian-style bathing costumes at the seaside.

 Write limericks about people you know.

JULY

 Pick the hottest day of the year to go ice skating in a sequinned one-piece.

 Ride down the stairs in a sleeping bag – wear plenty of padding!

 Pretend you're in a car and order a meal at a drive-through. Make it authentic by winding down the window and taking off your seatbelt.

 Change your phone's ringtone to a loud belch.

The best way to make your audience laugh is to start laughing at yourself.

Oliver Goldsmith

Laughing makes everything easier.

Carmen Electra

21 Don the skimpiest Speedos you can find and play a dramatic game of beach volleyball.

 22 Throw a party where everyone must come as their favourite biscuit. Better still, hire a pool so everyone gets a dunking.

 23 Chase a squirrel up a tree.

 24 Balance a spoon on your nose.

25 Try stilt-walking and other circus skills at a circus workshop.

 26 Throw a rope ladder out of a first-floor window and use it to depart the house in the morning. Make sure all the neighbours are watching.

 27 Be a superhero! Purchase a superhero costume and change into it in the nearest phone box, then perform a charitable deed.

 28 Ask out someone you like by tying a banner to a bridge that they drive or walk under every day to work.

JULY

 Using a large tarpaulin and plenty of water, create a water slide in your garden for after-dinner entertainment.

 Eat a foot-long hot dog.

 Spin on your office chair at high speed and shout 'wheeeeeeeeeeeeeeee!'

AUGUST

1 Get up really early and go down to the beach and create some giant footprints in the sand. Then hide and wait to see how people react.

2 Set the new email sound on your colleagues' computers to a sheep bleating, a cow mooing and a cockerel crowing, so it sounds like you're in the countryside. Hand out corn stalks to chew on to add to the effect.

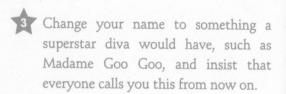 Change your name to something a superstar diva would have, such as Madame Goo Goo, and insist that everyone calls you this from now on.

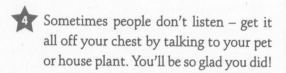 Sometimes people don't listen – get it all off your chest by talking to your pet or house plant. You'll be so glad you did!

On a rainy day, hark back to when you were younger and build yourself a den in your lounge or bedroom. Make it as sophisticated as you like, with cushions for walls, a hi-tech alarm system of bells on a string, fingerprint technology to open the door – the sky's the limit. Don't forget the *'Death comes to all who enter here!'* sign too.

 Applaud your work colleague when they have finished speaking at a meeting. Ask for an encore!

Laughter made you live better and longer.

Gail Parent

8

A sense of humour is good
for you. Have you ever
heard of a laughing hyena
with heartburn?

Bob Hope

9 Have an office chair race.

 10 Sing your responses to any questions that you're asked today.

 11 Put on a different accent to every person you speak to and see if they notice.

 12 Instead of making a cake for a friend's birthday, make a large wobbly jelly.

Take a water pistol out and about with you to cool off unsuspecting friends.

 Get those Christmas cards sent out early – do it now.

 Purchase matching outfits for you and your pet.

 Spin on the spot five times and then try to run in a straight line.

Pick a warm day and have a water fight in the garden. Be inventive with your water receptacles: buckets, wellies, watering cans…

 Mummify yourself with toilet paper and make monster noises as you exit the bathroom.

Teach a niece/nephew/child of a friend a ridiculous untruth. *'Chocolate has feelings.'* *'Cats like to wear pyjamas at bedtime...'*

 Backcomb your hair for the next important function that you attend. Some hairstyles are too good to slip out of fashion!

Nothing to me feels
as good as laughing
incredibly hard.

Steve Carell

Laughing brains are more absorbent.

Alton Brown

AUGUST

 Host a gurning competition in the pub.

 Go to a roller disco wearing the smallest crop top and your hair up in a side bunch.

 Go trout tickling – a friendlier and funnier way of catching fish.

26 See how many jokes you can tell in a minute.

 27 Help create the mood before watching your favourite film. If it's *Titanic*, build your own prow on the edge of your sofa so that you can recreate the iconic 'I'm flying' scene.

 28 Make your own crop circle by rolling around on a field. Photograph the end result and try to get it featured on the local news.

Go to a petting zoo and make friends with the animals – see if they will laugh at your jokes.

 Have a cake crawl with your best mate round the finest cafes in the area.

 Host an impromptu dance-off at lunchtime with your colleagues.

SEPTEMBER

 Wear black tie to dinner at the fast-food outlet of your choice.

 Eat dinner in pitch-darkness and see how much mess you can make.

 Go zorbing.

The most wasted of all days is one without laughter.

E. E. Cummings

With mirth and laughter let old wrinkles come.

William Shakespeare

6 Harvest your grape crop and make your own wine by crushing them with your feet.

 7 Hide from your partner/flatmate before they arrive home and jump out at them.

 8 Take a wig for a walk and claim it's a new breed of dog.

SEPTEMBER

 9 Wear fluorescent colours to work and mutter the words 'health and safety' when anyone asks about your choice of attire.

 10 Blow bubbles with bubblegum until it pops and sticks to your face.

 11 Buy some bizarre-looking vegetables – try finding a potato that looks like a three-legged man.

Put down a large sheet of paper, cover yourself with paint and become a human brush.

 Write a love song about your favourite chocolate bar. Upload it onto YouTube and see how many hits you get.

 Climb a tree and make wild animal noises when people walk past.

Sing really badly – and with emotion – while in the shower.

 Next time you're having your hair cut, invent a new, more outrageous you and tell your hairdresser all about your make-believe life. Be as convincing as possible.

 Learn to play the guitar with your teeth, like the late, great Jimi Hendrix.

Like all young men I set out to be a genius, but mercifully laughter intervened.

Lawrence Durrell

Laughter is the tonic, the relief, the surcease from pain.

Charlie Chaplin

20 Start a conga line at the supermarket checkout.

 21 Play on all the apparatus at the local children's playground.

 22 Twerk your way round the house.

 23 Work on your best impersonations and perform them for your friends.

Critique and review today's packed lunch and email your verdict to your co-workers, be sure to include stars for taste, service and ambience.

 Put food colouring in the milk to make breakfast time a bit more fun.

 Have a friendly arm-wrestle with your partner to get the day off to a good start.

 Arrive at work early and gift-wrap your colleagues' work stationery.

28 Learn to belly dance.

 29 Seed-bomb the greyest parts of town and take delight when you see flowers sprouting in the most unlikely places.

 30 Do cartwheels around someone who's waiting in a public place.

OCTOBER

 Autumn is in full swing. Make the most of the conker harvest by resolving your next disagreement with a fierce game of conkers.

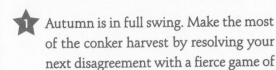 Get your apple-bobbing head on and prepare to get soaked.

 When sowing bulbs in the garden for the new season, plant them out so they make a word – could be a naughty word or simply 'hello'.

Laughter is an instant vacation.

Milton Berle

You can't deny laughter;
when it comes, it plops
down in your favourite
chair and stays as long
as it wants.

Stephen King

6 Wear a tail and ears for the day. Why should squirrels have all the fun?

 7 Take a ferret for a walk.

 8 Paint hens' eggs and claim they're real dinosaur eggs.

 9 Form a one-man band.

 10 Embrace the new school year and go to work wearing a smart outfit, satchel, and a shiny new pair of patent leather shoes.

Start knitting those Christmas jumpers. Remember to include your pets!

 Show your allegiance to your work and get the company logo tattooed on your arm – it doesn't have to be real.

 Take part in a nude calendar photo shoot – for charity, of course.

 Perform an impromptu stand-up routine while waiting for the bus. See how many people you can make laugh before the bus arrives.

One should take good care not to grow wise for so great a pleasure of life as laughter.

Joseph Addison

A wonderful thing about true laughter is that it just destroys any kind of system of dividing people.

John Cleese

17 Relive your childhood and buy some pick 'n' mix sweets, then have a sugar-induced crazy half hour.

18 When visiting a stately home, be sure to have a swing on a chandelier!

19 Pretend you're a hedgehog and snuffle your way through the autumn leaves.

20 Go foraging for mushrooms and try to come up with as many corny puns as possible: *'I'm such a funghi.' 'There's not mushroom in here.'*

21 Go speed-dating dressed as a frog and claim you have been bewitched and that only a kiss from someone incredibly attractive will break the spell.

 22 Walk backwards for the whole day – it's harder than you think.

 23 Challenge everyone to an arm-wrestle when an important decision needs to be made.

 24 Make a mudman – it's like a snowman but it's made of mud.

Have a conversation with a horse.

 Try to say a joke every hour on the hour for the entire day.

 Make lightsabres out of empty toilet roll tubes and fight for the good of the universe with them.

 Walk up an escalator the opposite way to its direction.

Get the giggles in a public place or meeting and see how long it takes to spread.

 Browse the autobiographies in the library or a bookshop and pick one by a comedian or comic actor that you admire and learn more about them.

Halloween: It's time for ghosts and ghouls and things that go bump in the night. Give your partner/housemates a good scare (and a laugh!) by dressing in drag.

NOVEMBER

1 Now the clocks have gone back, have an impromptu game of wink murder to liven up an eerily dark afternoon.

2 Record people saying their favourite jokes. Play it back when you need a bit of a lift.

3 Learn to unicycle.

See how many silly walks you can come up with during a brisk walk round the park.

 Bonfire Night: Don't let this special evening pass without a firework display. Purchase some indoor fireworks and invite your colleagues to watch the spectacle at your desk.

 Speak in pig Latin for the whole day.

If love is the treasure, laughter is the key.

Yakov Smirnoff

Laughter is the sensation
of feeling good all over
and showing it principally
in one place.

Josh Billings

Learn some funny songs and sing them on long car journeys.

 Using finger paints, draw your self-portrait and give it pride of place on the fridge. If anyone asks, say the cat painted it.

 Time to book that trip to the pantomime – invite the whole family so that you can all laugh together.

The next time you get an unwanted sales call, make animal noises down the phone – dolphin clicks are particularly effective.

 Lunge every time you stop by a colleague's desk before addressing them.

 See how many friends you can squeeze into an old-fashioned phone box.

Seven days without laughter makes one weak.

Mort Walker

Nobody ever died of laughter.

Max Beerbohm

17 Sew up the head hole of your partner's oldest jumper and video them as they try to put it on.

 18 Start creating gifts for friends and family. Make misshapen and ugly ornaments, and insist they are given pride of place in their homes.

 19 Illuminate the outside of your house with as many Christmas lights as you can get your hands on – claim that you want your house to be seen from space!

NOVEMBER

 20 Grin at everyone you walk past today and see if they grin back.

 21 Pay a surprise visit to a friend or relative you haven't seen for a while and take some classic comedy films that you can watch together.

 22 Go to a comedy club and watch the latest up-and-coming talent.

 23 Adopt the stance of a frightened hedgehog, curling up into a ball, the next time you are asked to do something you don't want to do.

Recreate the nativity for the family's Christmas card this year. The youngest family member must dress as the baby Jesus regardless of whether they are one or eighteen years old.

 Write the most ridiculous round robin letter to accompany your Christmas cards.

 If the ground is wet, have a worm-charming competition.

27 Recreate the iconic Morecambe and Wise 'Breakfast Sketch' when you have house guests.

 28 Sing a rock anthem (badly) into a friend's voicemail.

 29 Wait for the wettest, dreariest day, put on your raincoat and wellies and jump into every puddle.

 30 Become a kid again and build your own treehouse from scratch, then sit in it and eat sweets while reading comics.

DECEMBER

1 Pretend you're in a pantomime and disagree with everything you are told by saying, *'Oh no it isn't!'*

2 Walk round town eating an ice cream on this cold, wintery day.

3 Get into the Christmas spirit by attending a seasonal party dressed as a sprout.

Learn the techniques of a hypnotist. Begin by hypnotising your partner so they think it's always their turn to make the tea, then try to hypnotise a group of people into performing the cancan when you click your fingers.

 Set up an obstacle course in the office and time everyone as they negotiate their way round. Have a prize-giving ceremony and make medals out of foil to honour those with the fastest times.

Hearty laughter is a good way to jog internally without having to go outdoors.

Norman Cousins

Laughter is a tranquiliser with no side effects.

Arnold H. Glasow

DECEMBER

 Channel the spirit of Ebenezer Scrooge and shout 'Humbug!' at everyone you meet, before kindly handing out humbugs.

 Compose a fun seasonal song, but not a classic carol. Inject personal anecdotes, like the time you set fire to the dining table when you doused the Christmas pudding with too much brandy...

 If it has snowed, build an igloo in the garden.

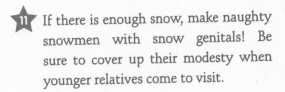

11 If there is enough snow, make naughty snowmen with snow genitals! Be sure to cover up their modesty when younger relatives come to visit.

12 Have a mock-Oscars ceremony with your friends to mark the end of the year. Give prizes for the biggest drama queen, most comical person and the biggest grump.

13 Wear odd shoes to a Christmas function – Helena Bonham Carter does it, so it will either be regarded as the height of fashion, or you'll be laughed at.

The sound of laughter is
like the vaulted dome of
a temple of happiness.

Milan Kundera

Laughter is the closest distance between two people.

Victor Borge

Make paper chains out of old work reports and strew them round the office.

 Dance like no one's watching at the Christmas party.

 Get a group of friends together and go Christmas carolling, but make that extra effort with your outfits and dress as a family of snowmen or Santa Claus's reindeer.

 Go sledging!

DECEMBER

 Decorate the Christmas tree with the contents of your underwear drawer.

Winter Solstice: Invite all your friends over, put on some cheesy tunes, wear your ugliest jumpers and make the most of the shortest day of the year.

 Try to nibble the gingerbread hanging on the Christmas tree without using your hands.

Make your own Christmas crackers. Insert the best jokes you have heard all year.

 Settle down to watch *The Snowman* on TV and join in when 'Walking in the Air' starts up by sucking helium and singing at the top of your voice.

Christmas Day: Hire a snow machine to ensure that your family wakes up to a white Christmas. If you're feeling particularly Christmassy, get the snow machine working inside the house too.

DECEMBER

 26 Wrap yourself up as a parcel and deposit yourself on the doorstep of a friend or relative that you haven't seen in a while.

 27 Serve snow for dessert with toffee sauce on top. Avoid the yellow snow though – it might taste funny.

 28 Make snow angels in the garden.

29 Read through the entries in your laughter journal and giggle at all the funny things that happened this year.

 30 It may seem a long time until summer, so why not recreate it in your house? Crank up the heating, lay out some beach towels, inflate a beach ball and pull on your swimming costume – voilà! Invite your mates round for a summer party on New Year's Eve!

There is nothing worth the
wear of winning,
But laughter and the love
of friends.

Hilaire Belloc

If you're interested in finding out more about our books, find us on Facebook at **Summersdale Publishers** and follow us on Twitter at **@Summersdale**.

www.summersdale.com